her white tree...

her white tree...

on releasing the shame and growing
our sacred...

by terri st. cloud

bone sigh books

ISBN: 978-0-9815440-8-3

bone sigh books

www.BoneSighArts.com

www.BoneSighBooks.com

Cover art by Noah Urban

www.BFGproductions.com

TABLE OF CONTENTS

~~~

There's a ramble here.

And a sigh (bone sigh) there.

And another bone sigh over here.

And more rambling over on that page.

On and on she goes...in no particular order.

Mixing rambling and sighing all over the pages.

holiness
~~~

and she honored the holiness inside her...

i don't know your name,
i only know a tiny part of your story.
a part that grabbed my heart
and insisted i offer what was inside of me.

this is for you.
this is because of you.
even tho we have never met.
it doesn't seem to matter.

this is an attempt to honor your scars
and to tell you i believe in your strength.

it is a holding of the sacred.
yours.
mine.
ours.

and a reminder that
no one
can take the sacred away
from us.

no one.

even if you can't see the sacred right now,
it doesn't mean it's not there.
and sometimes
it's the job of others
to hold it for you until you can see it.

this is both a holding and an offering...
with all that i have.

for you.

I didn't start out on this journey wanting to reach out to women and girls. I started out trying to find a way to support myself and my sons. That was it. Feed them, heat the house, pay the bills. It was all sort of a fluke, one of those weird things that you have no idea is going to happen, but then you look back and somehow know that you found the stuff that drives you. You somehow know that what looked like an accident wasn't an accident at all. And you somehow know that you have no choice left but to offer all of who you are and to reach out as much as you can - because there is no other way for you anymore.

And that's why I'm here. I'm a writer, poet, artist - sort of. It's a long story of how I got here, but here I am. There's a name for the things I create. I call them 'bone sighs.' Bone Sighs are quotes that I write that sometimes get put to art, sometimes not. I make them into prints or books or journals or greeting cards, or just leave them be as a plain ol' quotes. The bone sighs travel a lot. I sell them to stores, catalogs, on line, they're in women's shelters, hospices, healing centers and therapy rooms. Somehow, almost magically, they find their way to places that seem to need them. It's a process that amazes me, humbles me, and honors me. And through it all, I get to hear many stories, stories of the women that the bone sighs have somehow touched.

With every story, I try to hold what's going on. My reactions to the stories cover a wide range. Many, many times I close my eyes, bow my head, and just feel gratitude for being allowed to share another's journey.

And then, sometimes, a story will move me so much that I HAVE to create something. And that's what this book is. It's a reaction to a story. It's a dive deeper into my heart to try reaching out and touching my fingers to another, to grab their hands and hold on tight and let them know they aren't alone. It's my way of holding a precious young girl in my heart and wrapping her in gentleness and love.

I heard of this girl through a friend. She was giving me a brief outline of what happened. She was being discrete and protecting the girl's privacy so she didn't tell me much. What my friend wanted me to know was that the girl had been in tremendous pain, and that some of the quotes I have written touched her. She definitely had my attention, the tears were rolling down my face as I listened.

Her story is one like so many others. Trying to get over the horrible experience of being raped, she had to deal with the fact that the man responsible was out walking around her town. How many women and girls have lived this? I can't even imagine the terror involved in that. Feeling unable to cope, she found herself suicidal and in the hospital. Somewhere along the line, she was handed some of my writing and found something that touched her. And that's why the story was being shared with me.

I imagined this girl struggling so much, feeling so alone and scared and all the difficult things that had to be going on inside of her. And it was then that I knew I wanted to put something together for her and for every girl and woman out there struggling with this kind of pain. My heart was screaming at me to do it, and I know to listen when the pull is that strong. I did hesitate though. My self doubts began chiming in. I have never experienced the horror of rape. Who am I to try to offer help? I was molested as a child, but in the scale of things that girls and women experience every day, my experience didn't hold the weight that I felt someone who wanted to offer help should hold.

The doubts were starting to make a lot of sense. But then I'd think of that girl. I didn't even know her name, and yet, I couldn't get her out of my mind. And when I thought about the bone sighs touching her in a way she needed at that moment, I would hear my heart screaming all over again. And I knew I would listen. And that's how I got here. There have been internal arguments over intruding on her space that's already been so violated, arguments to stay quiet or to not explain how this book came about. But that seemed wrong to me. This book is created with nothing but love. The intentions are pure. And I'm going to believe that is the very reason I have to offer it.

I want to be very clear that I don't have the credentials I think I should have to help. And after a great deal of thinking, I've come to understand that this isn't 'that kind' of help. I can't tell anyone how to heal, or how to put down things that seem impossible to put down. Or really much of anything. What I can do is share my heart, share my writings, and share parts of my own journey with my own struggles. And that's it.

Something that my journey with bone sighs has taught me - and I'm not sure I would have believed this if I didn't see it for myself - is that even though the circumstances and events

9

may be very different in our lives, the emotions are the same. The struggles with pain, shame, feelings of brokenness, fear, lack of trust, and all the things we wrestle with are the same. We'll deal with it all differently, we'll take different routes to get to places we want to get to, we'll stress over different parts of it all, but the emotions we feel will be the same.

Some of the experiences are so much worse than others. I understand that, and hold that with great respect. It is to the feelings I speak here. As far as speaking to the experiences themselves, I can only bow my head, and hold that pain along side of you, with you. And remind you that you're not alone and there are so many of us out here who care.

Somewhere out there is a young girl who will never know how much her story moved me. She'll never know what she inspired. She'll never know how she touched me. And that's the thing, isn't it? We don't know how our stories affect others. We don't know what it is we offer just by living our stories and struggling to survive. But we offer so much, whether we know it or not. And that's something to think about and hold on to. Our stories matter. We matter. And you matter.

everything
~~~

*i give you my heart –
sometimes i think it's just not enough.
and then sometimes i know it's everything.*

a patchwork
~~~

how can people care
when they've barely touched lives?
ahh...but how can they not?
do the strands of connections
weaken because we haven't met?
or do they shine in all their glory
because of that?
you are out there somewhere
in the middle of your struggles,
your pain,
and your beauty –
and i am with you.

the healing began
~~~

feeling dirty,
ashamed
and damaged,
she hid her story.
not knowing that the woman next to her
also hid hers.
and the next woman.
and the next.
finally someone whispered the truth.
and their eyes met,
and their tears came,
their heads nodded softly,
and their arms reached out.
holding each other gently,
telling their stories,
the healing began.

When I feel really full of emotions with something going on inside of me, I sit and write. That's where the bone sighs are born - in the overwhelm of emotions. In thinking of the young girl I had just heard about, I knew I needed to grab some quiet time. Sitting myself down with pen and paper, four bone sighs poured out of me. It was as if they were just waiting for me to pick up that pen.

As I sat back and read them, I could see the influence of the last ten years of my life and the things I've come to believe about the process of our healing and growth running through them.

splinters
~~~

she built her cathedral
from the splinters of her
shattering.

So many women carry the scars of some sort of sexual trauma inside of them. As a matter of fact, out of all the women I have ever spoken with, only TWO have told me they have no such story in their past. And yet we hold these stories close, keeping them secret, never telling anyone. Or waiting years and years to finally whisper the faintest detail to another. More than once I've heard 'You are the first person I ever shared this with.' from a woman over forty. How could she carry her wounds alone for all that time and never share her truth? Is it because of shame? Shame is one heck of a powerful force.

We need to tell our stories, for many reasons. One of those reasons may be one you have never thought of before - in your telling your story, you give another woman space and permission to tell hers. You hand a key to a shaky hand that so badly needs to unlock those hidden doors inside herself. You actually help release another by telling your story. And in sharing these stories, I believe we create a starting place for healing to begin. Sharing stories creates keys of many kinds.

it wasn't hers
~~~

until she saw that it wasn't hers,
she wouldn't be able to put it down.
and with the way it crawled all over her
and covered her,
that seemed impossible to even imagine.
and yet, it REALLY wasn't hers.
she hadn't done anything wrong.
it wasn't hers.
her work would be to believe that.
it would take all her strength
and then some.
and when she found that knowing –
then she'd finally put it down.

Shame. It's wild stuff. We've all got it for a thousand different reasons. Coming in waves, it can rush in so strongly with such force that it's hard to believe we can ever get a handle on it. Where does it come from? Sometimes I wish I had an in-depth knowledge of psychology. I would really like to know why so often we feel shame for things that we aren't responsible for. How can we feel it so, so, so deeply when it's really not ours? Why do we take it and own it? Why do we take it and do that with it? I have no understanding of why we own it, but I certainly have a first hand understanding of actually doing that. I know this one well.

With my own shame, it always, always hits the "I'm not good enough" stuff. If I had been better in some form, I would have stopped it, or it wouldn't have happened in the first place, or I would have handled it differently. I'm talking shame in ALL areas of my life. It doesn't even have to be sexual. It can be in ANY area. And none of my shame stories are stories that I want to share. Throw in the sex deal, and it's over. No way do I want to talk about it. And yet, here I am, claiming that the world needs these stories. That we need to start telling them.

Here's one of the many, many reasons I think so. I truly believe in the message of the quote, 'it wasn't hers.' The thing is though, HOW do we figure out it's not ours? Do we just keep telling ourselves over and over it's not ours? Yeah, I think we need to do that. But I don't think that's enough. I think we need lots of angles and different things to work with and do. I think that hearing other people's stories teaches us about our own stories. If your girlfriend came to you and told you that she'd been attacked, would you for one second blame her for it? Of course not. You would hear her story, listen to her pain and want to hold her and comfort her. We can learn so much from those reactions. We can start turning those reactions onto ourselves. We can look at others' stories and see more clearly. Then with practice, we can turn that seeing onto ourselves. And then we can learn to offer ourselves compassion and love.

It's a double whammy right there. We can support other women and be there for them, AND learn to do the same for ourselves. I just don't think being compassionate to ourselves is something we naturally do. We have to learn it and relearn it over and over again. And we have to be patient and gentle with ourselves when we forget. Which is another thing I don't think comes naturally for most of us.

gently wrapping her
~~~

how do i tell her this isn't her fault?
how do i tell her it doesn't take her beauty away?
how do i tell her she matters and she's NOT damaged?
she can't hear me thru her sobbing.
...
thinking of women everywhere,
of their strength
and their survival,
i hold their power in my heart,
closing my eyes,
i wrap that power quietly around her,
and i sit and wait.

I am sincerely awed by the power of women. The stories that I hear and read and the strengths that flow through those stories leave me so proud to be a woman. And so many times these women who show such courageous strength don't even know that they have done so! They claim to just be doing what they needed to do to get through. And yes, I get that - to a point. But that's not all there is to it. Not by a long shot.

And women all over the earth, all through the ages have shown this strength. I would doubt very much that it's a strength that just pops up right away and fuels them forward. I'm sure much shaking, trembling and self doubt is mixed up in the beginning, if not all the way through the process.

I think that's important to remember and hold on to. When we feel broken or beaten, there's just no way we feel like a warrior. When all we want to do is sleep or hide from the world, or just stop the pain that is inside of us, don't even let anyone come by and try to explain about all this strength we supposedly have inside us. Just leave us alone.

And yet, it's not really alone that we want to be, is it? We want so badly to be understood and held and loved. If we're really, really lucky, we'll have people there doing that with us. We may not be very gracious about it either. Again, I wish I had the in-depth understanding of the crazy things we do. Why on earth do we push the people away that we really want close? Why do we sometimes make it almost impossible for them to be there for us? Again, I have no idea why, but know that it's real easy to do.

If you're lucky enough to have people that love you right there, maybe that's the place to put your effort. In letting them in. They need it as badly as you do. If you can't make the effort for yourself, maybe you can make the effort for them. Maybe that can be enough to give you the extra umph you need. Maybe just tell them you're lost and you're not sure why you keep pushing them away. Maybe just tell them that you want them close and you don't know how to make that happen. Maybe that's all you need to do to start. And that right there takes a whole lot of courage. And that right there can help so much.

And what if you're not so lucky to have people right close by? I'm thinking that any kind of shame stuff is so deep and so difficult, that we need to find some sort of support - therapy, support groups, that kind of thing. But we have to do that finding of these things on our own. We have to find the strength to go get what we need. And the whole idea of doing that on our own sure stinks.

I've had some stuff that I've had to deal with on my own in my life. And it felt like a really lousy deal. At the time nothing felt good about it. But later on, looking back, I realized I had gotten a crash course in a whole lot of important things that way. Including self love. I think that's the way it works. Those really hard things totally suck - and at the same time, there's little bits of gold we pick up along the way that we don't even know about until later. We look back and think 'Wow, look what I did.' And that's a way cool moment.

It's just that when it's happening, it's really, really hard.

Whichever way it works for us, having people next to us or our finding ourselves alone, and I guess it works different ways all throughout life, I think it helps to remember that strength just doesn't pop on in and have us running around fixing all our problems. It can creep in slowly...so slowly that we don't even notice. And for the times we don't think we have any strength at all, we can kind of hang on to other women's strength and wrap ourselves in that.

silver linings
~~~

i walked thru hell
and burned my soul...
part of me lost forever.
grieving,
i found the others.
burnt and charred like me.
holding on to each other,
i knew -
even hell had a silver lining.

energies
~~~

sharing their power,
they help me find mine.

echoes
~~~

the sorrow was so deep
it echoed in places that seemed untouchable.
it was to those places that friends' love seeped.
so slowly and ever so gently,
their love quieted the echo.

layers
~~~

she was the first layer.
with layers inside layers.
her tears opening fold after fold.
infinity inside one.

they were the next layer.
women the world over.
their pain sending tremors thru
the very fabric of the earth.
one inside infinity.

dancing and falling.
rising and crumbling.
digging deeper and farther.
weaving dignity and honor.
layer after layer.
infinity becomes one.
one becomes infinity.

more than anything
~~~

more than anything –
i want to trust a journey
that i don't understand.

The way I figure out stuff inside myself is by stumbling into it, or over it, or on top of it. I'll land there somehow and think 'Oohhhhhhh look what I found!' Early on in my personal searching, I figured out that I didn't really believe that I mattered. I don't even know how I figured that out. I guess I started listening to what I was saying and feeling. Some things become obvious when you start listening. And then when I wrote this bone sigh called "i matter" - well, it was hard to ignore what was going on inside of me.

i matter
~~~

it was when she first dared to see her truth,
that the winds howled.
after a time, it strengthened her
and she spoke her truth
and the earth shook.
and when finally,
she believed her truth–
the stars rejoiced,
the universe opened,
and even her bones sang her song:
"I Matter!"

I had started noticing that people who told me I mattered didn't back that up with their actions. When it came right down to it, I didn't matter. That is a hard thing to discover. And true to that crazy-makes-no-sense-why-we-do-it way of thinking, I figured it was because deep, deep down, I really wasn't loveable and somehow it was all my fault. That is typical for me. Something's wrong? Well, it must be something I've done or didn't do. Sound familiar?

Okay, so why do we do that? Why are someone else's lousy actions our fault?! But they were. For awhile anyway. I did a lot of digging around inside myself, and I did a whole lot of trying to see myself, and just a whole lot of work. And things started to change. I saw how I carried some of that belief deep inside of me. The belief that I didn't matter. I carried it and allowed that belief to surround me.

Interestingly, one day out of the blue, it hit me that the day I was molested as a little girl was the day the message that I didn't matter really got burned into me. Then I think I got that message over and over again. But I truly believe that's when it originally got sunk way down deep inside of me. How could I have mattered for that man to have done that?

And life goes on and on. Looking back, I find many different times where I can ask similar questions. How could they have done that if I had mattered? Wouldn't they have been different to me if I had really mattered to them? On and on in a thousand different ways we can come up with questions like that.

And then one day, it finally, finally started to dawn on me that these things weren't about me. They were about THEM. They did these things for their own reasons. Not for mine.

grace
~~~

maybe grace is figuring out
it's not all about you.
that people are doing what they're doing
for their own reasons.
not yours.
and maybe grace is accepting that.

21

So intellectually, I could kind of hold that idea. Someone would do something that hurt and I would think over and over, "This isn't about me. This is about them." Well, yeah, it sounds all nice and neat, but it takes a long time to really, really have that sink in. But you know what? It started to. It really did. Especially when I started really seeing the other people.

"Seeing" had been an idea that had grabbed me and really caught my attention. I was sure that if I could see who I really was, I would regain the power that I had lost along the way. Thing is, I think it's a matter of not just seeing yourself, but seeing the others as well. It all seems so entangled somehow.

And HOW do you start seeing yourself for real? How do you start seeing others? I think it takes a lot of work, practice, understanding and acceptance. Acceptance that we've all got issues, and those issues can control a lot of things. Understanding that other people's issues have controlled them and in the process, hurt us. And then looking at our own things that control our own selves and working with that stuff so we can step out of that control and really understand what's happening inside of us. When we can see clearer how we work, we can be clearer on what's happening around us.

And THAT part is up to us. THAT'S what we need to own. That's the part that now becomes our deal. If we're going to make the decision to really look, what are we going to do with what it is we see? Life isn't handing us situation after situation to tell us we don't matter. It doesn't work that way. Others are doing what they're doing for their own reasons. We are too. And what ARE our reasons for what we do? If WE believe we matter, are we acting like it? That's a big one to look at. And if we don't believe we matter, what's up with that? What has such a tight grip on us that it's blocking that? It's a lot to look at. And no, I guess we never really have to look. But then I wonder, what will we miss if we don't?

your truth
~~~

it is your truth.
your power.
your soul.
guard it with all you have.
don't let anyone's misconceptions steal it.
including your own.

seeing
~~~

the power lies in the seeing.
until she could see herself
with her own eyes,
she would not regain her power.

back to life
~~~

weeping tears of recognition,
she found herself among the ruins
and brought herself back to Life.

I spent so much time trying to see myself and getting nowhere. It drove me crazy. At one point, I gave up and decided that if it was that hard for me to see myself, maybe I just didn't really need to do it. And that's when it seemed that the seeing began. Maybe it was the giving up of trying so hard that helped, I don't know. I mean, how do you ever really know how far along you are with the whole process of seeing yourself? If you could see you'd know, but how do you know if you're really seeing? Oh, it can get confusing. But something happened anyway. I look back at this road that I've traveled, and know that I see way more of myself than I ever have before. And I trust myself enough now to not fight myself so much in the process.

That sentence is a big one. 'I trust myself enough now to NOT fight myself so much in the process.'

That's been a long time coming. And honestly, I don't always have that down. But this whole trusting in myself and working with myself - why was that something that felt so foreign to begin with?

Way early on in my search, the man who was to later become my partner said something to me that hit really deep. He told me that he clearly saw that I needed to forgive some things inside myself.

Whew. I remember where I was when he said that. Thankfully, he wasn't in the room with me, he was on the phone. I wasn't ready for him to see the tears that came to my eyes when he told me that. There was truth in what he said. That thought inspired one of my earliest bone sighs called 'forgiveness.'

forgiveness
~~~

she reached as deep as she could
inside her pain.
somewhere in there was a piece
of herself she needed to forgive.
and only then would her healing be complete.

Again, nice words...lovely thought...but my gosh, one heck of a job to actually do. And also again, it's the kind of thing that can feel hard and impossible when you're going through it, but it's the kind of thing that will bring you gold. And just digging in and trying to start with that leads into so many other things that need work too. It wasn't long before I was in a darn avalanche of inner work!

herself
~~~

she'd been fighting herself so long now,
the idea of trusting herself seemed foreign.
and yet...if she could trust...
if she could just trust herself ~
she just might discover the best
friend she's ever known.

her giant
~~~

she called upon the different parts of
herself for help.
if she was going to make it,
she needed to accept them all,
unite them all,
and believe in them all.
it was time for a huddle of
tremendous proportions.
it was the making of her giant.

in
~~~

she was scared again.
seems she was scared a lot
these days.
time for a deep breath
and another plunge in.
it was the only way to get to where
she wanted to go.
so, in she went.

somehow
~~~

'it's entirely up to me,' she thought.
terror filled her.
but she'd do it anyway.
because somehow she could.

time
~~~

it was time to let go of her fear
and embrace her strength.

let's go
~~~

trembling, she opened her heart,
quietly, she whispered,
'let's go.'

My own dark periods have been pieces of cake compared to a whole lot of people reading this book. But they were dark for me, and they were the times I felt cut off from everyone. I was sure no one really understood and no one could really see who I was. If they could, they'd see that I really was damaged goods and that I was beyond repair.

I knew that. They didn't. But I did. So their words, while nice, were meaningless.

What a completely alone place to be.

I'm not so sure that in the end, that's a bad place to be. For just a little while anyway.

I mean, I really don't ever want to be there again. I won't ever wish it on anyone else. And yet, if you're there, I feel some sense of hope for you. Yeah, I really do. I've watched it over and over and over again. With what I do, I hear a lot of hard stories. I see a lot of people walk through their own hell. And I see the change that can happen there. I have seen the transformations take place. And sometimes I wonder if the really deep transformations only happen in the fires of hell. I have no idea - but I do know some powerful stuff happens there.

rough roads
~~~

you've been down a rough road, my friend.
did you preserve your heart of gold
thru the fires you've been thru?
or did those fires burn it brighter?

We forget when we're down there in that pit, or even if reminded, we don't believe it or care. It seems like it might not be until we're on our way out of the pit that we can look back and see that something has changed us, we've traveled far, and we're different, in a profound way.

down deep
~~~

going down deep
she screamed to the stars -
direct me!
guide me!
lead me!
pull me!
get me beyond me!
filling with their light,
she came up once more -
ready to live again.

the Light
~~~

finding the crack of light,
she pried her fingers in its edges.
pulling the darkness back
with all her strength,
the ocean of light poured forth.
weeping tears of gratitude,
she felt the Light flood over her

It really wasn't until I was forty that I started seriously searching and looking for healing. Seems like by the time you hit forty that you'd know a thing or two. Hmmm...it really surprised me the things I didn't know and the false beliefs I carried around so easily. Looking back now, I shake my head at some of the things I had to put down. And with ten years having passed, I can see why it's taken me so long to travel. It's like I had to start from the bottom up. I know there's a long, long way to go still ahead of me. But I'm okay with that as there's no question in my mind now that what I'm gaining along the way is worth the effort.

One of the most basic things I carried around with me was the belief that good always wins. That love can conquer anything, and that Light beat Darkness every time. Looking at that now, I wonder what planet I was on. How could I have gone forty years, watched the world spin around and still believe that? But I did. It wasn't that I didn't see the darkness win before, I think it was just that I didn't want to accept that idea. So I just sort of made up a theory that worked for me that was based on Disney movies or something. How crazy is that?

It took watching a traumatic event in a friend's life to get that belief blown out of me. It knocked any sort of pretending that I did so far out of me that I knew it'd never be back. I saw that love didn't win. Even when it was right and just that it should have. And then, as if Life wanted to make sure that I understood the point, two more traumatic events happened in my own life.

Standing in the chaos, I knew that the belief in good always winning was gone. And at the same time, I realized other beliefs were no longer working for me and other things I had been pretending about were also gone. I stood there empty handed wondering what on earth I did believe in.

perhaps
~~~

perhaps power is letting go
of the grip of the past
and standing empty handed
facing the future.

32

I pictured standing at a cave's entrance. I don't really know where it was supposed to be. In my depths, I guess. A sacred place where only I could go to. I went into the darkness and saw it glowing inside. I could see the floor. Taking all the beliefs I had left, I threw them all over the cave floor. I didn't know what I believed in any more and I didn't want to hold all this 'stuff.' Let the cave hold it for awhile.

My plan was to leave it all lying there on the floor, hoping that the things that really mattered to me would come back to me. The other stuff could just stay in the dark cave. I didn't want to hold what other people told me was right any longer. I only wanted to hold things I truly believed in. And I wasn't sure what that was, and I wasn't sure how long it would take for me to figure it out, or even if I ever would, but I knew I had to let go of what I had been holding.

I even threw my version of God into that cave. I let everything go.

The following bone sigh is written after I found the god part in my life again, the 'you' in the quote is god.

silence
~~~

i looked for you in their stories
and i couldn't find you there.
i looked for you in my own stories
and lost you there.
crying, i released all parts of you
and waited in silence.
wondering if i'd ever see you again.
wondering if i'd ever touch you again.
slowly, you crept back into my being.
slowly, i understood you never left.
quietly, i watched.
quietly, i felt.
trembling, i stood in awe.
trembling, i bowed my head
as your presence filled me.

That bone sigh wasn't written right away. Not at all. It took a long time for me to feel anything again. I'm still on my journey in finding the beliefs that will either come back to me, or find me for the first time. I think it may be a life long process.

I had thought that I held on to trust the whole time. That I couldn't have started that whole cave process unless I held trust in my heart. That maybe that was one thing I just never let go of and didn't realize it. But I don't think that's true. I think I was in such a desperate spot that I had no idea what would come back and what would never return and I just couldn't care any more. All I knew was that I couldn't keep going like I was going.

And once again, I believe that there are times when desperation is the only vehicle that will take us where we need to go.

an understanding
~~~

it was an understanding that found its way to her.
she understood now.
it had sunk in.
good wasn't always going to win.
she understood that all too well.
but that's not why you keep trying.
you keep trying because you have to.
you keep trying because if you don't
the dark really will always win.
and that isn't an option.
you keep trying because your heart
can't live any other way.
you keep trying because that is your way of living.
you keep trying because ultimately,
you believe in light.
because ultimately,
you believe.

maps
~~~

there is no map.
you gotta write your own.
you gotta carve your own.
you gotta sweat, cry, grieve,
laugh, and love your own.
and when you're all done,
that's all that will have mattered.

I remember hanging up the phone one night after talking to a friend. The sound of the phone hanging up exactly coincided with a feeling I felt inside of me; it was a feeling that something just snapped in half. My friend had been swimming down in the depths of some of the darkest of the dark waters we can swim in. I had been trying to hang out along the edges with her and let her know she wasn't alone. I'd been on the sidelines for awhile when we came upon this phone call together. She'd been drinking and was a lot more free with the things she was telling me.

The pain in her voice cut right through the phone lines and seared into my veins. I held my head as I listened to her and tried to stay present. I heard how her pain was creating her reality. It was loud and clear. It made me crazy. I fought the desire to try to correct her and tell her that reality didn't have to be that way. I knew that she needed a safe place to vent. I wanted to offer her what she needed. And I knew that she would not be able to hear me that night. And so I stayed quiet and present.

When I hung up the phone, I felt the snap. I sat staring out the window. And then I grabbed my pen and paper and wrote my heart out. The bone sigh 'for women everywhere' was born.

for women everywhere

something snapped inside of her.
'ENOUGH ALREADY' she screamed.
it's time for women everywhere to
claim their worth, their value,
their beauty, their sacredness.
no more of this believing the darkness that's been
thrust upon them.
no more taking the blame for the sins of others.
no more claiming themselves failures
when in fact, they are survivors.
it's time for women to stop.
turn around.
face those people who have hurt,
harmed and wounded and let them know
that they refuse to be destroyed.
they refuse to carry the burden.
it's time for women everywhere to
claim their power,
their beauty and their right to shine.
it's time for women everywhere to
place the palms of their hands on
their wounds, acknowledge the pain
and change the world with the lessons
gained from that pain.
it's time to move with the wisdom
of a survivor and to know your strength.
the world is waiting for us.
let us step up now and reclaim ourselves,
and reclaim the world.

There's a whole lot of ways we give our power away. And it doesn't even have to stem from some traumatic event in our life. It can be learned from the way we're raised, it can be because of our lack of belief in ourselves, it can be because of many different reasons. We all do it at different times, some of us more than others, some of us without even realizing we're doing it. We give away our power, and we take whatever reality is being handed to us.

Something I love though, is that for just as many reasons that we give our power away, there are that many and more reasons that we find to start taking it back. It starts out small, and then grows and grows and grows.

commitment

it is in the commitment to trust
that mountains begin to move.
it is the commitment to love,
that walls begin to crumble,
and it is in the commitment to one's self
that worlds unimagined begin to become real.

One of the most powerful moments of my life is burned into my memory. It happened in the ugliness that can come in the midst of a marriage splitting apart. I had told my husband that I wanted a divorce. He was hurt and angry. Not knowing what to do, he verbally lashed out at me over and over again. And in my own confusion and not knowing what to do, I took those lashings over and over again. On one of the nights when he was at his worst, he focused on every vulnerable spot I had and he attacked those spots with a verbal vengeance. With each attack, no matter how slanted and skewed it was, I still took at least a tiny piece of it as true. It was in the very beginning of my searching, and I was so raw and new to the whole journey. I just didn't have the strength to throw the garbage down. I think I needed to punish myself in some sense as much as he did. So with each jab, some part of me accepted that I 'deserved' what he said. Some part of me took it and believed things that were completely wrong about myself. I took his vengeance and allowed it to override my own truths.

Until...until...until he hit the subject of 'bone sighs.'
I had just begun my journey into writing the bone sighs. They were born in my pain, they were raw, they were my depths, they were me. There wasn't one grain of doubt inside of me about that. I knew that with every fiber of my being. They were the real that I had been missing my whole life.

He made the mistake of attacking them. It may have been one of the most powerful things he could have ever done for me. Because when he went there, I knew he was completely wrong. I knew he didn't know what he was talking about.

And I knew that I knew the truth.

I could believe in the bone sighs unlike anything else inside of myself. They had been born to me out of my darkness, they were mine, no one else's, and they were me. And I believed whole-heartedly in them! That was the first time ever that I believed that deeply in myself.

I remember crouching over on the ground, just curled up on the log I had been sitting on, taking it all, and then he went there. I remember my world stopped right then. He kept going, but I stopped there. Looking at the ground, I thought "He's wrong! He's so completely wrong!" I let him keep ranting. I turned my thoughts to my sons and how I could take care of them through this horrible mess. I put the revelation of that moment on hold. And then later that night, when everything was quiet, I went back and took it out of my pocket and looked at it again. And held it with complete amazement.

It turns out that moment would be held and looked at many times over. It would be the moment that I would use to help myself believe in myself. It would be the moment that helped to give me my power back.

her power
~~~

she took her power back ~
without permission.

I know there's no telling when these moments will come. And I know that there's absolutely no telling any one else when they should grab these moments. They come in the oddest forms at the oddest times. I'd just like to be a reminder that they do come. And we can and will grab them when we least expect it. And sometimes when we're feeling really weak and beat, we still grab them and we don't even know that we have done so until later.

a sister
~~~

she sits alone
hurting in the dark.
not ready to reach for the candle i offer.
blowing it out,
i sit down next to her and wait.
we'll light the candle together
when she's ready.
for now,
i'll trust the darkness for us both
and sit quietly beside her -
letting her know she's not alone.
letting her know that darkness is okay.
letting her know that i'm there,
waiting,
with a candle.

There's so much to this hard stuff. So many layers, so many strings, so many different things pulling on us or burying us or confusing us.

I look back at my own hard stuff. The layers involved. There's the big layer, and maybe, in a way, it's really the only layer. I don't know. Maybe all the other layers are different forms of the one big one? I'm not sure. But the big one for me is the mattering deal. If I understand that I matter, if I really grasp that I count and I'm valuable and worthy, then everything starts to change.

The other things I think I would throw in there as more strings and layers are things like trust. For example, learning to trust the process of life. That one thing right there involves seeing that life isn't always pretty. Life is complicated and hard. How do you trust something that's complicated and hard? And then I see that if you really boiled those thoughts down, you'd probably be talking about trusting yourself. Trusting yourself to handle what life throws your way. Trusting yourself to grow and become stronger and not crumble under the weight of things, and to take those things and make something inside of yourself with them. Do you trust yourself that much?

Trusting of life also brings in your beliefs about life, about a higher power, about the meaning of it all, your whole spiritual and philosophical outlook. Yet another string, and no small string at all. More like one heck of a rope.

The trust stuff brings in the idea of friends and relationships. What is it you believe about that stuff. And yeah, it's easy to see how the mattering stuff is tangled up in that.

There's the whole 'inner child' subject. I love the idea of us having an inner child. I understand that many people don't feel the same way about it as I do and would prefer to leave that whole concept on the curb. For me, it's one of great interest and one I like to explore. It brings up different threads too though. How is your childhood stuff affecting you? How do you treat the different parts of yourself? Do you even believe you have different parts to yourself? And if you do, how does that help you work with yourself? And how does it muddle things up for you?

Oh my gosh, the threads and twists and turns and opportunities to get muddled abound. And yet, I think it's sort of beautiful too - how complicated and intricate we are. While at times that can just feel overwhelming, I think it can be terribly exciting too. There's so much to ourselves. So much we can work with. Get stuck in one part, go to another. Start to see your beauty in one part, you can bring it to another.

I think maybe it all begins with just trying to hold the things we know. And yes, that includes our sorrows and sufferings as well as our strengths. I believe that the holding of the tough stuff creates some amazing muscles. And sometimes we need those muscles for us to be able to release our grasp of things that need letting go. It seems to be an amazing dance of knowing what to hold on to and knowing what to let go of.

a thought
~~~

you can't let go of what you haven't held.

open hands
~~~

she wasn't holding the sorrow.
it was holding her.
turning towards it, she opened her hands
and let it rest inside her grasp.

a vow to my heart
~~~

i will work on the act of listening to you
and my listening abilities will grow.
i will honor those things you relay to me
and act upon them.
when i act upon them, i will know that
i am living my truth and owe no explanations
to anyone.
i will believe in your ability to accept all emotions
and will not close down to protect you.
i will direct my energies and my power
to places that will strengthen you, not deplete you.
i will follow you in the way i wish
the world would follow you.
the child of the universe
and the heart
shall meld
and we shall dance as one.

me, myself
~~~

i commit to me, myself, today.
i vow to listen to and follow
and believe in my goodness.
to recognize my strength
and wield it with the added power
of compassion.
to know my heart
and trust it
and not turn to outside expectations
to feed it,
but rather, turn to my own inner guidance
to lead me.
to know that i am the woman i want to be
and work to uncover more of my beauty daily.
and to be gentle with myself when i slip –
loving myself even in the darkness.
to me, myself, i give my love.
and it is from me, myself, my love is returned.

And just like the incredible mix of things that confuse and muddle us on our journey, there are the whoppers of things that will just stop us in our tracks. And they don't come small do they? There's fear, and anger and rage and old habits that won't die and struggles with believing in ourselves. All that stuff. Oh my gosh. No wonder we have to keep stopping and reminding ourselves to trust.

Anger is a fascinating subject. And one I am not qualified to write about. I just know from some of my own wanderings into it, around it and through it that there's a whole lot to anger. I really think we can use it for a tool at times to push ourselves forward. And that it can be a good, healthy thing to work with. And yet, that can be a tricky one, because if you hang on to it too long, it won't work anymore. It becomes the burden that keeps us from growing. It can be helpful in how we see and understand things, and then it can blind us so that we can't see any good anywhere. It is a tremendously tricky balancing act.

Speaking of tricky balancing acts, how about figuring out who you're really mad at or what it is you're really mad at? Sometimes it seems so obvious. And yet other times I think it can be confusing. I know I've thought I've been mad at someone before, when it turns out I'm more mad with me. Or I'm not really mad at all, I'm really scared and the anger covers that up and keeps me distracted.

I wonder how much of anger is really based on fear?

And then, fear! Oh my gosh, I think I'm an expert on fear! I feel that mixed in a whole lot of my life. And that is equally as fascinating. When I walk through my fears and try to find out what exactly I'm afraid of, it can be hard to figure out. I'm amazed at the amount of times it boils down to fear of myself. Fear that I can't handle something that may happen. Where in the world did I get that fear from? I guess from being hurt and not wanting the hurt to happen again, and not feeling like I can handle it if it happens again. And then I think I make everything crazier than ever in my head by taking these things and running with them and exaggerating them. That's definitely a habit of mine, which directly ties into those old habits that won't die that I mentioned above.

it's there
~~~

it's there.
inside you.
yeah, it's easy to forget –
to get discouraged and distracted.
but go back again.
because it's there.
waiting for you.
inside you.
your strength.
your wisdom
and your peace are there.
inside you.

the light inside
~~~

when things were hard
and when it hurt,
she closed her eyes –
searching for the light inside.
slowly, it brightened enough
for her to see it.
quietly, she felt it –
touched it –
held it.
and steadily it warmed her.
and softened her once again.

One very deep habit I have, I think, is to run to fear for all kinds of things. You know how you have all those default settings on a computer? Things it just naturally lands on and goes to? I think I have one of those - a fear default setting. It's like a habit. If I'm not sure what to do, I'll be scared.

I have a whole bunch of bone sighs dealing with all these topics because it's something I wrestle with a lot. I want to include them here in case they're something you wrestle with too. And I'd like to add that it's real easy to see what we do wrong - how we run to fear so fast, or how we can hang on too long to anger, or any of that stuff. And it's not so easy to see what it is that we're doing right. But we ARE doing stuff right. We can tell just because we're thinking about this stuff. Just thinking about this stuff is a big step. And trying to figure ourselves out is so important. There's all this tiny stuff that we do that's not so tiny. We just don't see it, but it's there, and it's bringing us to where we want to go. Maybe it feels way too slow, and like we'll never climb out of the darn hole we're in. But we're climbing, and it matters.

keeping her strong
~~~

she was scared.
to trust seemed an enormous task.
she held onto her friends
and let their trust
keep her steady -
and let their love keep her strong.

her light
~~~

anger boiled inside of her,
strong and furious.
reasons to lash out ran thru her head.
arguments not to countered them.
tension, frustration and tears filled her.
and the the words came...
'my soul is my own.'
suddenly the target of her anger lost its power.
she would give it no more.
she turned away
and moved towards her Light.

I walked with someone who was going through her darkness. Sometimes when I use the word 'darkness' I want to stop and say 'Wait a minute, do you know what I mean by that?? Do you REALLY get how black the blackness was of the darkest night she was going through??' And then I think, yeah, you probably do. No, I probably don't need to explain it. Her stuff was darker than anything I had encountered personally. I didn't know how to help her. I was just filled with the idea that I couldn't let her walk it alone. And that even if I didn't know what to do to help her, I'd at least be fumbling by her side. I would hold love next to her and just try my hardest to keep some sense of love present.

I watched. And I wondered. How does anyone come back from this cliff? How does anyone find their way back to any sense of light? How could anything ever grow inside her again?

I have no answer as to how it happened, I can only tell you what I witnessed. In places where I thought there could never be life again, I saw stirrings. It made me think of a documentary I had watched years and years ago. It was about what happened to the land after a volcano had covered it with lava and ash. I only remember one thing from that show so many years ago...I remember the video shot of green shoots of life coming up thru the hardened black lava. That visual came to me over and over again as I watched my friend begin to come back to life.

shoots of light
~~~

it wasn't total darkness.
she had thought it was.
the blackness had blinded her to the
shoots of light that broke forth.
eventually tho, she did see them,
those shoots of light.
placing them in her heart,
she used their light again and
again and again.

a tiny glow
~~~

at first it was all blackness.
dark and deep.
then the light cut thru,
shooting a spark her way.
turning, she looked.
felt.
smiled.
allowed.
the blackness faded,
the depths warmed,
and a tiny glow began to grow.

playing it safe
~~~

the fear won't help you save what you have –
it will make you lose what you could become.

＊

the pain
~~~

the pain had stopped her too many times.
taking the form of fear,
it gripped her tight.
but now, her belief became more important
than her pain.
turning towards it,
she allowed it to fill her.

＊

i will not run
~~~

i will accept my falls
embrace my scars.
live my passion.
i will not run.

When I was hurting really badly, the way I wanted to cope was to drink. Just drink and numb the pain and get through what I had to get through. But I had kids. I was a stay at home/ home schooling mom. That whole plan of drinking wasn't going to work for me. I don't think it works for anyone, really. But that didn't mean I didn't want to anyway. But I knew I had to stay completely away from that desire, so I decided to go in the other direction. I decided that instead of drinking and numbing myself, I would pay attention to everything that went on inside of me. Talk about opposites! Oh yeah, Terri, let's not numb anything, let's go for FEELING everything! Great, Terri, let's plow into what you want to avoid. Crazy. But I did. I decided I was going to explore it.

Way easier said than done. Sometimes the pain just got to be too much to hold. I didn't know what to do with it. I didn't know how to cope with it all. And that's when I turned to writing. That's how the bone sighs were born. I would write when it was too much to hold. And I would pour the pain out on the paper. At least enough to give me some sort of release.

At one point, when I just figured the writing wasn't doing enough and that a drink would help, I had to sit through that feeling. It was so strong. It was pulling on me so deeply. One little drink. It would just help so much. I stalled. And I hung on. I literally sat there and hung on to my chair until the desire for a drink went away. And then I wrote about it! That was quite a feeling of empowerment. Here's what came from that moment -

voices
~~~

the pull was calling again.
so strongly it called her.
no.
she didn't want to answer it...
and yet...
she stalled.
give it enough time.
it will pass.
'stall.' she told herself.
'you can do it.'
the voices in her head going back and forth,
the struggle intense, the moments magnified.
and then slowly, the call weakened.
the spirit strengthened.
she stepped forward with relief and pride.
she was moving on –
with an even stronger spirit
and a stronger body.

the fist
~~~

and the fist became the open hand.
she refused to beat herself any longer.
speaking words of kindness,
she gently touched her hair,
looked into her own eyes
and took the first step towards love.

continuing on
~~~

almost crumbling to the ground,
she stopped.
looking at how far she had traveled
and all it had taken to get there,
she recognized her strength.
the strengths she had inside of her,
the strength she had gained along the way -
her inner power.
standing tall,
she faced forward and continued on.

I think that writing is tremendously helpful. And it's something any one of us can do. You don't need to have anything but a piece of paper and a pencil. You don't need to 'know how' to write. I never considered myself a writer. I still don't. I write a whole lot, but writers are people who are famous or know what they're doing or know grammar or can at least spell. I'm not a writer. So what? I write anyway. And the good thing about not knowing what you're doing is that you don't have to follow any rules because you don't know the rules! That makes it a lot easier, I think. You don't need to be a writer to write.

Something I did naturally without even realizing what I was doing was I used the words 'she' and 'her' when I referred to myself. That helped a lot. And I didn't even know why. Someone later pointed out to me that it was like the pain was too much for me to claim so I had to put it on another person. Bam! That totally hit me when she said that. I do believe that's true. And I think that's such a cool thing to know. Why not try it? And if it feels too much to use your own name or the pronoun 'I' - use she, her, another name...anything. There are no rules.

The idea is to have a healthy place to go to where you can get some of that stuff out when it just gets too darn big to hold.

And sometimes that place can end up being a place where you find yourself without even realizing you were looking.

new keys
~~~

the new door wouldn't open
with the old key -
she found scrubbing the key
wasn't enough.
she needed a brand new one.

There was a time when the heavy feelings just went on and on and on and on. I felt like life had come and put these big, heavy, gray woolen blankets on top of me. One at a time. Over and over again. One on top of another. I felt so weighted down and so drab, no color anywhere inside of me and gray wrapped all around the outside.

I did all the things I had to do to keep my life moving along, but there was no lightness to any of it. There was no color. That's what stood out the most for me - the steady, heavy weight and the lack of color.

One day I was working under my house doing some home maintenance project. It was a big deal for me to go down there as I'm claustrophobic. But it had to be done, and so I went. I had finished up and was heading out of the crawl space. I was on my belly, pulling myself out, half under my house and half outside the little crawl space door. I just stopped right there, halfway between worlds and looked up at the sky. "Help me," I said out loud. Some- how it had just landed on me right that second that I couldn't get out of this slump that I was in on my own and I needed some help. Right there, that moment, out of the blue, I asked for help.

No, I don't know who exactly I was asking for help. I'm not religious and I'm not sure what my spiritual views really are, but I did have a sense that I just needed to throw this out there to some bigger force than just me. And looking back, I just love where I was when I did it. It seems so symbolic to me now. I don't know if I figure the house was me or the weight of the world or what - but I love the fact that I was laying in the dirt, fighting my fears to be there, stopped somewhere halfway out and halfway in, between two worlds with this big structure sitting right over me.

Does something really happen when you finally release, fall back and ask for help? Yeah, I think it does. I really do. Now, I can't tell you what. Does a God hear your cry? Does a universe that flows a certain way ripple over your words and start flowing in a different direction? Does the act of crying out and releasing open your heart to new doors? I have no idea. But I do believe something happens when you really, truly release. And it was then, after that, that I could feel the colors slowly coming back.

No, they didn't come back right away or all at once or in some kind of massive wave of color. They came back just enough to stir my wanting more of them. They came back enough for me to really remember what it was that I was missing. They came back enough to get things rolling inside of me, enough to make a spot for the colors to grow again.

And they did grow. And eventually, they did come back. And when I'd feel them, I would know what a gift they were. And sometimes they'd leave again. But I would hold on to the fact that they had started to show up again. And that I really wanted life with color - not this gray gunk. And I would look for that color and hold it as much as I could.

the first notes
~~~

hearing the first notes inside herself,
her eyes got wide.
growing louder and stronger,
colors began mixing with the sounds.
holding on tight and letting go all at once,
she stepped back into the dance.

making space
~~~

it is in the act of allowing good things to come
that lives are transformed.

maybe it's time
~~~

maybe it's time to take care of yourself.
maybe it's time to scream out loud
that you don't have the answers
and you just plain can't figure out what it's all about...
but you're in this for the full ride.
maybe it's time to stop doin' the half ride.
maybe it's time to step into it all.
to weep your guts out.
to hurt all the way to your core.
to allow that hurt to be there.
maybe it's time to embrace the love
and believe in it even tho it's not always perfect...
but it is always right.
maybe it's time to shout out to your depths
that you do matter
and you will do all in your power to live healthy.
maybe it's time to stop just getting thru,
just surviving.
maybe it's time to grab the gift you've been given
and celebrate every single piece of it -
including the pain that brought you here.
maybe it's time.

forget the maybe...and know it...
it is time.

i want
~~~

i want to really really live.
i want to laugh til my stomach tightens so much
that it aches and my legs hurt from my slapping them.
i want to cry from my gut and let the tears wash me
to where i need to go.
i want to hear the singing of my heart,
and let the sounds echo inside me
and i want to dance to that music.
i want to fill with compassion and touch
someone's face so gently that they can feel
the caring in my fingertips.
i want to love so deeply that my cells vibrate with it
and just standing near me you can feel the buzz
of the vibrations.
i want to know that i'm worthy and i'm good
and i want to leave self doubt on the highway.
i want to touch the sky and recognize my soul in it.
i want to walk in the rain and drop to my knees
in gratitude for this gift of life i have been given.
may i never ever forget what a gift it truly is.

I had no idea how visual I was until I started writing bone sighs. From them I could see that I picture things in my head all the time. Water is a huge theme with me. Rivers running through me, wells deep inside of me, oceans and waves and drips and floods. So many water visuals.

Caves are another one that come up a lot. Sacred places deep inside of me that only I can enter. Places that hold my sacred, and also hold the garbage that I've collected over the years. I can safely leave the garbage in those caves.

And the most recent theme is one of stars. Imagining that I am filled with stars. That stars can run through me. I can picture stars in my veins, or in my heart, or resting in my hair. I've sprinkled stars around other people when they've been in darkness, or just plain forgotten that they have stars inside them too.

All this visualizing is something that I do naturally. I can't believe it took my getting into my forties for me to see that I work visually and it's a great tool to help me.

I know a lot of other people out there are visual too, so I wanted to bring this up. And if you're not visual, maybe you can figure out which tools you use inside you to cope with things and figure things out. It's odd that we're not taught to look for these tools we use. But we're not. It's up to us to find them.

river of steel
~~~

plunging her hands deep into the mire,
she touched her river of steel.
shoving the muck out of the way,
she let its silver waters cleanse her.

her cathedral
~~~

she kneeled at the cave entrance –
hands had quietly removed the snow and ice
that had blocked her view.
lit in warmth and sacredness
she gazed upon her cathedral.

remembering
~~~

she's a child of the universe.
filled with laughter and stars and goodness and
sparkles.
tho sometimes she forgets.
the world gets dark,
feels lonely and heavy.
until the winds come with their reminders,
touching her face, touching her heart.
closing her eyes, she remembers.
opening her eyes, she smiles.
and the stars shine bright once more.

I remember the first time I used a visualization as a tool to help myself. It was late in the night. Everyone was asleep except me. I was in the middle of some of my dark stuff and just couldn't sleep. Laying there feeling a tremendous amount of pain, I tried to remind myself that I wanted to explore this stuff. That I had told myself that I would go wander through the hard stuff and look at it. Yeah, but this was too hard. It hurt so bad I just didn't know what to do. I honestly didn't feel like I could endure the pain.

Without even knowing what I was doing, I closed my eyes. I felt the pain. I felt where the pain was sitting. It was in my heart. There was no mistaking where it was. It hurt so badly. I felt about out of my mind with the pain. 'Okay, what do I do with this?' I asked myself.

I was a mom at this point. I had three sons and knew how to help them with their hurts. So I thought of that. What is it we do when someone gets hurt? I pictured my heart and I held it in my hands. I pictured holding it with both of my hands and walking over to my kitchen table. I put it right on the table. (I know! What can I say? It wasn't gross as I did it in my mind, but sounds pretty bad as I write about it. Bear with me, though, these visualizations seem to have their own set of rules.)

At this point in my life, I was using something called 'tea tree oil' for scrapes and cuts the kids were getting. We used it for so many different things we teased that it was magic and it could heal anything. And so as I lay my heart down on the table, I looked at it with gentleness and compassion and asked, 'What would be tea tree oil for my heart?'

The answer came easily and without hesitation - 'Friends.' And I understood that my tendency was to isolate myself when I was struggling, but that what I needed to help my heart right now was to surround it with people I trusted and loved. 'Spend some time with your friends.' I heard that, and I respected what I heard. I understood that some sort of internal wisdom was speaking to me and I wasn't taking it lightly.

I also understood that there was help that I needed right inside of me. Guidance. I picked up the pad of paper by my bed, and wrote the bone sigh called 'home.'

home
~~~

her ache echoed inside of her,
stirring her inner voice.
it was then that she remembered
she wasn't alone –
and once again,
she turned inward towards home.

And then the next day, I called my friend and asked if we could meet up. It turns out that she was to become vital to my survival. To this day, I choke up every time I try to describe what it is she did for me. It was her words that told me I wasn't crazy, it was the looks she gave me when I tried to describe what was going on around me that told me I really wasn't losing my mind.

I think that I normally would have tried to go it alone. I would have tried to ride it all out by myself and not let anyone in. I am so grateful for having listened to that voice inside me that spoke to me on that painful night.

And for anyone hesitating about letting someone else in like that, turns out that I did make it out of those days and I found strength I didn't know I had. And then, when someone else near me landed in their own nightmare, I understood the value of someone's presence, and I paid back what I had been given. She has since told me several times that my being present saved her life. Nodding through my tears, I knew just what she meant.

Lean, take what you need, get stronger. And then give it back to the world. You will hold a compassion and understanding and depth that only those who have been through the fires can offer.

holding the light of you
~~~

sometimes i didn't think i could do it.
other times i knew i had to.
the journey now was inward.
it was what was left to offer.
holding the light of you,
i enter my darkness.

together
~~~

standing in the middle of the chaos,
we hold on tight to each other.
knowing nothing for sure
except the love between us,
we go forward.

different directions
~~~

thrown in a different direction -
overwhelmed and grieving,
she covered her face.
one by one,
they came and held her,
encouraged her
and gave her hope.
uncovering her face
and leaning on their arms,
she walked her path.

Not long after stepping into the journey of trying to grow myself and find out more about myself, I heard about 'inner child' work. Three different people at three different times mentioned it to me. By the time the third person suggested this, I decided to pay attention and give this a whirl.

The basic theory (I think) is that we all have an inner child inside of us. Part of us that needs nurturing and healing. And that we can use different methods to get in touch with that part and work on healing some wounds that we carry around with us.

Having no clue as to what this all really meant, I asked someone how to get started. I was told to sit down quietly with a journal and write a question out with my dominant hand. And then with my non-dominant hand, write the answer. No editing, filtering or censoring, just write what came to me.

Sounded easy enough. And for me it was. I have since heard from others that this just didn't work for them. Again, I think it's because different tools work for different people. Each time I did it, I got results that intrigued me. And it always looked like a kid wrote it. The whole thing was freaky to me yet really exciting.

At some point I decided to try the visualizations with the part I had now come to refer to as 'Little Terri.' So on my morning walks, I began to picture her and talk with her. I think that's when I really stepped into the world of visualizing. It was easy for me, she would come right on out and talk with me. And these visuals had a magic life of their own. I didn't consciously guide them. I just went where they led.

There's so many different ways to access what's going on inside of us. It's just that it's scary and such new territory. If we can just begin to trust ourselves, to trust that we have an inner wisdom inside of us, I think that can open the doors closed within us.

inner wisdom
~~~

your inner voice is the voice of the soul...follow it.

67

my little girl
~~~

i went back and got her today.
the girl that is me.
i coaxed her to stand,
to drop the blanket,
and to pick up her beauty.
she's walking with me now,
and leading me to wholeness.

honoring my wholeness
~~~

always with me,
waiting inside.
sometimes quietly,
sometimes not.
it is when i stop and listen
that i honor your presence.
it is when i follow what i hear
that i honor my wholeness.

I've run with the whole visualization stuff and have talked to different parts of myself, seen women of the ages, and became intrigued with an image I call 'Butterfly Woman.' These visualizations have never scared me. It has been heavy and hard at times, but never scary. And sometimes it's just plain fun! I found this description of something that came to me one day, and I wanted to share it here.

The visualization is this: I am both the surgeon and the patient. My body is lying in front of me on the operating table, wide open and ready for anything. The surgeon, also myself, is yanking hard and strong on a fist full of veins she has in her grasp. Pulling hard and moving her arm sideways to make room for them to come out, she's dragging them loose speaking with conviction. 'We're gonna yank this whole darn system out. We're gonna replace it with a brand new system. Nurse! Bring me a new one! I want one that's clean, vibrant, star filled yet wide open, rarin' to hold a flow of good things, and not so good things. We need a brand new system! Double check the stars! That's important!'

'Look at the eyes here! These veils, these filters. They have got to be removed. And this build up on the heart? Oh my, time to scrape that out and help the beat. The lungs. Look under here. Gunk. Some nasty past history gunk that needs to be loosened so that the breathing can go much deeper. Someone hold up the manual so I can follow the schematic. Rewiring these veins is gonna take some concentration.'

"Light. I need more light. There you go. Right there. Steady now. Scalpel.'

It's been ten years. Ten years of trying to figure out what love is, how it works inside of me,
what it feels like when I touch it, and how it's connected to the flow of life. I have been hard
on myself, gentle with myself, ruthless with myself, compassionate with myself, bitter, grate-
ful, exhausted, excited, done, just beginning again, confused, sure, scared, confident, two
feet in, head under the covers.

Two days ago (from this moment that I'm writing this) I had the visual above. And it felt
glorious and exhausting all at once. The time has come. To some, the visualization of yank-
ing ones veins out can't be too comforting. For me, at this point, it feels so incredibly right.
I have done the prep work. I believe that. It's been ten years of prep work. Pre-op. Ten years
of pre-op. And I don't visualize the yanking out as the hard part. It's the rewiring that's go-
ing to take the concentration and effort.

~~~~~

I was pretty darn excited about that visual. It was so goofy and unusual and so full of zest. I
got a kick out of it. And I believe it got me thinking about 'rewiring' the things inside of me
which sparked the visual that this book is named for, the visual of my white tree. I found my
original writing on it and wanted to share that. I felt like if I rewrote it, I might lose some of
what it meant to me. What follows is the story that the title of this book is based on.

I came up with the color theory today. Actually, if we're going to be technical we could call
it the 'peri-menopausal color theory.' It goes something like this:

Let's suppose love is a color. And being the uniquely creative soul that I am, I picked red.
A nice, deep, rich red. Now, when we mix in our upbringings, the examples of love we've
grown up with, the movies, magazines and general cultural messages we receive with our
own experiences, we have what we believe is love. We walk around thinking that we under-
stand this thing, that we know it and that we live it. We think we have our dark, deep, rich
red. But what we really have is a washed out light pink. Oh yes, there's a few of us who have
worked a little bit harder, thought a little bit deeper, and now have a solid pink for our love.
And we think this is it. We think this is the red stuff.

I liken this to peri-menopause. The time that comes before menopause. The time that can go on and on and on where you exhibit some menopausal symptoms, you touch a form of it, you get an idea of it, but it's only a partial experience. It's not the real deal.

Peri-menopausal pink love. That's what I think a lot of us have. And that's absolutely okay if we know that and want that. It's a decision we all have to make for ourselves. But that's the thing. I'm not sure any of us ever makes a 'decision' about what we think love is. Well, a deeply thought out decision anyway. I think we just kind of wander into something and accept that as our truth and don't question it a whole lot.

Now, maybe I should stop for a moment here and mention that this love talk I'm doing isn't about romantic love. While that can be covered in the love deal, of course, it's not the entirety by any means. I mean love in all its forms, and definitely including self love.

Although, now that I mention it, a great place to observe some of your root systems is in a significant-other relationship. I watch a lot of my own stuff there. I believe in that watching, and in that safe space that's been provided for me to do that, I started seeing things about myself, things that are hard to see during other day to day relationships.

And lately, perhaps because of this whole rewiring decision that I made recently, maybe I gave some kind of inner permission for something different to take place inside of me. I don't know. All I know is I saw something in a way I had never seen before. In the past, I believed I had certain thoughts, certain theories of what influenced me, and yes, on certain days I would even say on what DROVE me. But I hadn't actually SEEN these things inside myself. It's one thing to know something is going on, it's an entirely different thing to see it.

And somehow the other day, without even trying, I saw it. It was a feeling, accompanied with a visual and also some sense of a knowing. I guess I should have thought 'How perfect. Just in time to include in the writing.' But I didn't. It freaked me out and scared the daylights out of me.

Here's what happened: I opened a door. Sort of an outside door and an inside door all at once. Picture opening a door that's standing in a door frame all by itself outside somewhere. You open it and your view is different. You see the great vastness of the outside and right in front of you is a burned, charred, demolished mess. Right at your feet. Ruins. And somehow, without a moment's hesitation, you know those ruins are your core. There's the sky and the clouds and this vastness all around. And there's embers and black stuff.

At first I thought it was a building, a demolished building. I thought my core was this building that got bombed or something. But in trying to describe this to my son, I realized I had it wrong. When I told him what it felt like with the door, and opening it and what I saw and how I guessed my core got that way from things others had said and done to me, he listened intently. When I was all done he puzzled over the picture. If the start of all this truly was from what other people had said and done to me, wouldn't it have been a building that was built in place of my core? Or around my core? Wouldn't it have been a building that others built for me and one that was now my job to tear down? He was confused with the visual. He saw it as people putting things on me (building the building) and hence there was a building that needed to fall. The logic wasn't working for him. He sincerely asked me about this.

And so I started thinking. I felt like I had been operating from the very same premise he was talking about for a long while. I hadn't really thought it out in words or visuals, but some general, vague feeling inside of me floated around with the idea that I had to knock down what other people had put in my way. But now I realized I was coming up with something different. His questioning it was making me really look.

In explaining to him, I realized it wasn't any building at all. Somehow I was just filled with a knowing, right there in the middle of the thinking. I stopped and paused. And I have to tell you, the relief inside of me was tremendous. Suddenly I understood it was a burnt tree, and it all tumbled inside of me and started to make sense.

'It's like we all come with this huge white tree,' I said to him. It was all landing in my head and feeling so right. I continued on with something like this: the huge white tree is us, our goodness, our potential, our true selves. We've all got it. Every single one of us. And yeah,

these trees get hacked, burned, carved, chopped, demolished - you name it. We all get stuff done to that tree. As I described this, it really hit me what I had seen in my visualizaion. Those were the ashes and ruin of my huge white tree.

I stopped in the middle of this explanation. It was taking my breath away. There's a big difference between a tree and a building. The tree is alive. Oh, yeah, it's been pretty much creamed. But there's still life there. There is. It's not an inanimate object like a building. I didn't need to find the bricks and mortar and beams. When I had thought I needed to round up these things to rebuild, I was completely lost. I didn't know where to get these things. I didn't know how to begin. I was completely lost and really, really scared.

The tree visual changed all that. Sure, it was demolished. And yeah, it was pretty darn burnt, black and well...basically gone. BUT! There was still life. You couldn't see it, but I knew it was still alive. It could grow again. It could sprout and come back. I understood that immediately. And the things it needed weren't things I would have to build and construct. It needed sunshine, and rain, and warm temperatures and nurturing. It needed natural things that would come and be there if I let them in. It needed me to provide a nurturing environment. I could do those things. It still wouldn't be easy. I thought of some of the struggles I have, and knew it still wouldn't be easy. But it was doable. I could see doing this. And with this new thought, everything inside of me changed.

It's one thing to see your core in complete ruin and know that you can grow it again. That's a pretty overwhelming visual. But to see it in ruins and think that you don't even know how to build it back or where to find the things to build - well that felt pretty hopeless.

And so now, I turned to a burned core feeling full of hope. The first thing I thought was that I needed to clear the ashes off. I needed to make room for the sun to find its way in. I needed to make room for growth to return.

Later that night, I closed my eyes and pictured the spot. On my hands and knees I pushed mounds of ashes and charred stuff off the spot. I scooted it over to different people I knew who had helped in the burning. 'Here, this is yours.' I said to the different people. I didn't stop and give them the evil eye. I didn't stop and throw the ashes in their faces. I just pushed it over to them, pronounced it theirs, not mine, and went back to work.

They weren't what mattered. They weren't where my focus was, my focus was on the tree.

I have a feeling this growth is going to take awhile. I want to get started on the growing stuff. I want to see that beautiful green sprout come up. I've got things to do and things to look forward to. The looking back stuff no longer interests me. I've done that already. For a long time. It is no longer my focus. My focus is now on growing.

her white tree
~~~

a tree of life.
a tree of knowledge.
a tree of soul.
a tree of goodness.
a tree of her.
it was her core.
burnt.
scarred.
hacked.
cut.
chopped.
and carved in.
it was still there.
it was still there!
pushing the ashes out of the way,
making room for sunlight
and water –
she nurtured it back to fullness,
she nurtured it back to life.
and she and her tree
held the sky and its moon
and together, they danced
and together, they grew.

The white tree visual was so powerful for me, it's truly helped so much in how I work with myself now. I wanted to offer it here to remind you that you have your own white tree. And you really can grow it. Even if it doesn't feel like it right now.

I want that to be the last thought I ramble about here. It truly feels like a worthwhile thought. So I will just leave it her for you.

When I started putting this book together, I gathered the bone sighs that I wanted to share here. I'd like to just share them now quietly. I'll place them on the pages that follow and hope that something you read will touch you, and maybe awaken the stirrings of your own white tree.

brave
~~~

maybe being brave is no more than
staring down the 'less than' feeling
and stepping up to the 'i am worthy' feeling.

underneath
~~~

her head ached.
her eyes were red.
and on the upper layer was exhaustion.
underneath tho,
there was a peace that steadied her.
she felt it,
trusted it,
and leaned towards it.

turning
~~~
she turned towards the trust
and stopped running.

unearthed
~~~

shovel full after shovel full,
she unearthed her self.
kneeling at the beauty
that had been buried,
she cleansed it with her tears
and lifted her self
into the Light.

back to life
~~~

weeping tears of recognition,
she found herself among the ruins
and brought herself back to Life.

exhilarating
~~~

freeing herself of the dust of her past
was exhausting.
who knew dust could be so heavy?
who knew the fresh air would be
so exhilarating?

she flew
~~~

having tired of the negative words -
she laid them down.
being finished with the weighted
boots,
she burned them.
touching a feather to her tears,
she slipped on her wings,
turned to her sky -
and flew.

high dive
~~~

it was a dive off a very high cliff –
into the depths below.
knowing it was her only chance at living,
she closed her eyes and dove
and trembled every bit of the way.

shaky landing

even after she landed,
she trembled.
wanting guarantees
and knowing there were none,
she vowed to keep diving
until guarantees
no longer mattered.

weaving
~~~

in and out
up and down
over and over
she wove her strands of life together.
patching hole after hole
eventually she saw it was more than
the threads that gave her strength,
it was in the very act of weaving itself,
that she became strong.

so much more
~~~

yes, there was sadness,
but there was so much more.
belief in herself.
strength that kept growing
and a knowing that she was okay.
and would always be okay.
no one could take that away now.

her beauty
~~~

i look at her and see beauty,
and yet, she's been told she's not beautiful.
i watch her and see love,
and yet, she's been told she's not lovely.
i want to shout to her
'you are precious beyond words!'
yet, i know she can't hear me.
and so i won't shout.
i will just keep believing in her
and reminding her.
and wait for her to see it,
to hear it,
and to know it
as deeply as i do.

journey of tears
~~~

sometimes it's a journey of tears.
and sometimes she'd forget and
block them.
but never for too long.
as they had a will of their own.
and then they'd flow.
and she'd feel relief.
and she'd remember again
that sometimes it's a journey of
tears.

dust
~~~

you, my child, are not throw away material.
you are made up of the
fabric of the universe –
threaded with the very dust of the stars.
know it.
accept it.
and allow it to shine forth.

the whole
~~~

she could never go back
and make some of the details
pretty.
all she could do
was move forward
and make the whole
beautiful.

drop it
~~~

drop it.
turn your back to it.
leave it behind.
we need your hands free.
we've got some digging to do
to find your light
that you lost along the way.
it's still there,
even tho you doubt it.
it's still there.
and we'll find it together.
and when we do,
we'll fall on our knees
in gratitude and joy.
we'll laugh.
we'll cry.
and then gently,
ever so gently,
we'll take it back out to the world.

she valued

~~~

and she valued herself.

a roar
~~~

hearing her pain,
she stood up and spoke out loud.
another heard.
another spoke.
forming a circle around the wounded,
they bared their scars to one another.
gently they whispered.
we are one.
we are not in this alone.
we are one.
the chant grew stronger.
and stronger.
and stronger.
until a roar shook the earth.
and the world listened.

souls
~~~

she didn't just survive –
she became.

You are not alone.

Reach out.

Find the others.

Find the tools inside you.

Don't let anyone take away who you are.

You are beautiful.

Go within and find your white tree.

You can do it.

You matter...
honor yourself...

if i could
~~~

if i could teach you anything –
it would be to
hear your heart,
and to know your beauty,
and to believe in
your possibilities.

Terri's a searcher and a ponderer who started her own business to raise her three sons as well as herself. Her sons are about raised. She's still trying to figure herself out though. And figures it very well may take a lifetime or more.

Want to learn more?

Come on over to bone sigh arts at www.BoneSighArts.com.
Or visit Terri's blog at www.BoneSighArts.blogspot.com.
Find more books at www.BoneSighBooks.com

Love the cover art?

Visit graphic designer, Noah Urban at www.BFGproductions.com